W9-DIO-503

Questions and Answers: Countries

Afghanistan

A Question and Answer Book

by Gillia M. Olson

Consultant:
Abdul Raheem Yaseer, Assistant Director
Center for Afghanistan Studies
University of Nebraska
Omaha, Nebraska

Capstone press

Mankato, Minnesota

Fact Finders is published by Capstone Press
151 Good Counsel Drive, P.O. Box 669, Mankato, Minnesota 56002
www.capstonepub.com

 Books published by Capstone Press are manufactured with paper
containing at least 10 percent post-consumer waste.

Library of Congress Cataloging-in-Publication Data
Olson, Gillia M.
    Afghanistan: a question and answer book / by Gillia M. Olson.
    p. cm.—(Fact finders. Questions and answers: Countries)
    Includes bibliographical references and index.
    ISBN-13: 978-0-7368-2685-3 (hardcover)
    ISBN-10: 0-7368-2685-8 (hardcover)
    1. Afghanistan—Juvenile literature. [1. Afghanistan.] I. Title. II. Series.
DS351.5.O45 2005b
958.1—dc22   2004021783

Summary: A brief introduction to Afghanistan, following a simple question-and-answer
    format that discusses land features, government, housing, transportation, industries,
    education, sports, art forms, holidays, food, and family life. Includes a map, fast facts,
    and charts.

Editorial Credits
Erika L. Shores, editor; Kia Adams, series designer; Jennifer Bergstrom, book designer;
    maps.com, map illustrator; Wanda Winch, photo researcher; Scott Thoms, photo editor;
    Eric Kudalis, product planning editor

Photo Credits
AP/EPA/Syed Jan Sabawoon, 9; Bruce Coleman Inc./John Elk III, 12–13, 21, 25; Corbis/AFP,
16, 16–17, 23; Corbis/Caroline Penn, 11; Corbis/Reuters NewMedia Inc., 19; Corbis/Ric
Ergenbright, cover (background); Corbis Sygma/Jacques Langevin, 27; Cory Langley/Teresa
Rerras, cover (foreground), 15; Courtesy of Gayle Zonnefeld, 29 (top); Getty Images
Inc./Hulton Archive, 7; Stockhaus Limited, 29 (bottom); Victor Englebert, 1, 4

Table of Contents

Features

Where is Afghanistan?

Afghanistan is a country in southern Asia. It is about the size of the U.S. state of Texas.

Mountains are Afghanistan's major landform. Mountains cover at least half of Afghanistan. The Hindu Kush mountain range runs across the middle of the country. In winter, snow falls in the mountains.

Rugged mountains cover much of Afghanistan's landscape. ▶

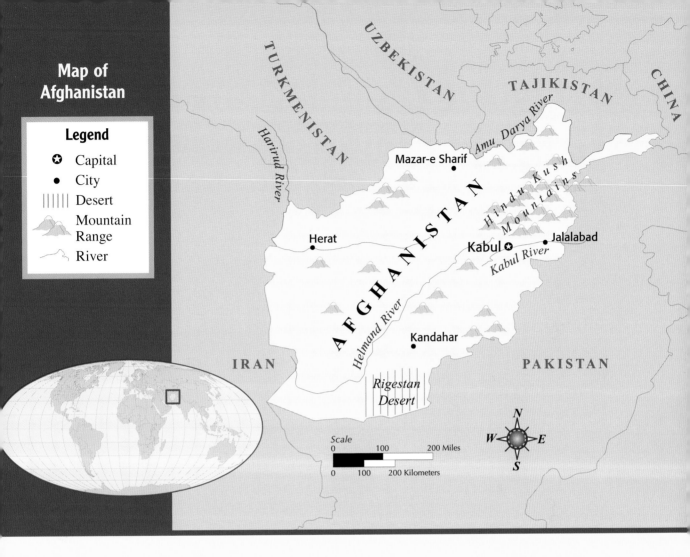

Map of Afghanistan

Legend
- ✪ Capital
- ● City
- ||||| Desert
- Mountain Range
- River

TURKMENISTAN

UZBEKISTAN

TAJIKISTAN

CHINA

Harirud River

Amu Darya River

● Mazar-e Sharif

AFGHANISTAN

Hindu Kush Mountains

● Herat

Kabul ✪ ● Jalalabad

Kabul River

Helmand River

● Kandahar

IRAN

PAKISTAN

Rigestan Desert

Scale
0   100   200 Miles
0   100   200 Kilometers

N W E S

Afghanistan's mountains divide the
northern plains from the southwestern **plateau**.
Most of the country's farming is done in the
northern plains. The Rigestan Desert is part
of the dry southwestern plateau.

When did Afghanistan become a country?

Many people believe Afghanistan became a country in 1747. During most of Afghanistan's history, invading groups ruled the area. In 1747, Ahmad Khan began ruling Afghanistan. He was a Pashtun, which is the largest **ethnic** group in Afghanistan.

Great Britain took control of Afghanistan in 1880. Over the next 13 years, Great Britain set the modern borders of Afghanistan.

Fact!

Shah is the Persian word for king. Ahmad Khan became Ahmad Shah after becoming king. He also used the title duri dawraan, meaning "pearl of the era." People called him Ahmad Shah Durrani.

Amanullah Khan passed Afghanistan's first constitution into law.

In August 1919, Afghans overthrew British rule. That year, Amanullah Khan passed the country's first **constitution**. Today, Afghans celebrate their Independence Day in August.

What type of government does Afghanistan have?

Afghanistan's present government came to power in 2002. It is a **transitional** government. The Taliban had ruled Afghanistan from 1996 to 2001. U.S. troops and another Afghan group overthrew the Taliban in late 2001.

Hamid Karzai heads the transitional government. Thirty other people advise Karzai. They represent education, finance, and other areas of government.

Fact!

The Taliban believed in very strict Islamic laws. Under the Taliban, men could not shave their beards. Women were forced to cover their faces and entire bodies in public.

Hamid Karzai (at the podium) is the temporary leader of Afghanistan.

A 1,600-member **Loya Jirga**, or grand council, set up the transitional government. Leaders from **ethnic** groups across the country took part in the Loya Jirga. In 2004, elections were planned to elect the country's leader and lawmakers.

What kind of housing does Afghanistan have?

Most Afghans live in mud-brick or concrete houses. In cities, some people live in apartments. Often, many related families live together in one large house. Each family has their own living space inside.

Where do people in Afghanistan live?

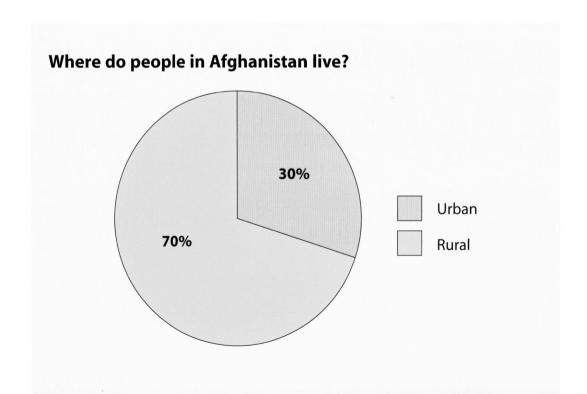

30%

70%

Urban

Rural

Families in Afghanistan often live in mud-brick homes.

Almost nine percent of Afghans are **nomads**. Most of the year, they live in one spot. During spring, they move their animal herds to new areas to feed. Nomads live in tents made of animal skins, wool, or cloth.

What are Afghanistan's forms of transportation?

Most people in Afghanistan do not own cars or trucks. Many Afghans ride colorfully decorated buses. People also walk or ride bicycles. People use carts pulled by horses to move goods and people on city streets. In rural areas, people often ride camels, donkeys, and horses.

Afghanistan has few paved roads and no usable railroads. Many Afghan roads were damaged by war bombings.

Fact!

The Khyber Pass allows people to travel through the mountains between Afghanistan and Pakistan. The pass is only 42 feet (13 meters) wide in one spot. Cars and trucks travel on the one paved road.

People travel through city streets in carts pulled by horses.

Afghanistan's major airport is located in its capital, Kabul. Ariana Airlines serves the airport, along with other international airlines. Some cities in Afghanistan have smaller airports.

What are Afghanistan's major industries?

Most Afghans work in agriculture. They raise crops and herd livestock. Many Afghans grow wheat, **barley**, corn, and rice to eat. Fruit, nut, and cotton farmers sell crops at local markets or to other countries. Afghan herders raise sheep for their wool and meat.

Mining is a small but growing **industry** in Afghanistan. Afghans have mined the rare lapis lazuli stone for hundreds of years.

What does Afghanistan import and export?	
Imports	*Exports*
food	fruit and nuts
manufactured goods	wool
textiles	woven carpets

Most Afghan farmers grow food to feed their families.

   In the last 20 years, people have begun to mine natural gas in the Hindu Kush valleys. Natural gas can be used to heat homes and provide electricity.

What is school like in Afghanistan?

Some schools in Afghanistan are taught by a mullah, or priest. They often meet in the village **mosque**. When the Taliban ruled, most students learned only the Koran. It is the holy book of Islam. Today, children learn reading, writing, science, and math.

Children read lessons written on blackboards in Afghan schools. ▶

Most students in Afghanistan learn to speak Pashto or Dari.

During the Taliban's rule, women were not allowed to work. Many women lost their jobs as teachers. The Taliban also kept girls from going to school. Today, many women have returned to teaching. Girls can attend school.

What are Afghanistan's favorite sports and games?

Buzkashi is Afghanistan's national sport. *Buzkashi* means "goat pulling." *Buzkashi* is a team sport played on horseback. The "ball" is a headless goat or calf. Teams score points by moving the headless animal to a goal area.

Kite fighting is another popular sport. In kite fighting, players cover kite strings with glue and glass. People try to fly their kites and cut the other players' kite strings.

Fact!

Buzkashi players usually train their horses for five years before they ride them in a buzkashi game.

Thousands of people sometimes attend buzkashi *games.*

Sports played around the world are also popular in Afghanistan. In cities, people can find soccer games and volleyball games. Boxing and wrestling are also popular.

What are the traditional art forms in Afghanistan?

Poetry and music are popular in Afghanistan. People combine these two art forms in storytelling. Families gather to tell stories. People pass on family history by telling folktales.

Afghans are known for their weaving skills. People around the world buy Afghan carpets. Most Afghan carpets are wool. They usually have red backgrounds and simple black patterns.

Fact!

Most Islamic art does not show people or animals. Many Islamic artists believe creation of people or animals should be left to God.

Colorful tilework decorates many of Afghanistan's mosques.

Many of Afghanistan's mosques have painted tilework. The blue-green tiles often show flowers and plants. Other tiles form patterns of circles, squares, and lines. The famous Blue Mosque in Mazar-e Sharif has fine examples of tilework.

What major holidays do people in Afghanistan celebrate?

Most Afghans are **Muslims** and celebrate Islamic holidays. The month of Ramadan is an important time for Muslims. Most people **fast** from sunup to sundown. At the end of the month, people have a feast called Eid al-Fitr.

Another important Islamic holiday is Eid al-Adhha. It honors the time when Abraham was willing to give his son to God. Because of Abraham's devotion, God allowed him to kill a ram instead.

What other holidays do people in Afghanistan celebrate?

Labor Day
Mawlid (Muhammad's birthday)
Remembrance Day for Martyrs and Disabled

During Eid al-Fitr, Afghan children play games to win prizes.

Afghans also celebrate non-Islamic holidays. Nowruz, New Year's Day, is celebrated on the first day of spring. During Nowruz, families attend fairs and have picnics. Jeshen is Independence Day. It is celebrated on August 19.

What are the traditional foods of Afghanistan?

Rice, naan, and yogurt are the main foods eaten by Afghans. Rice is served with beef or lamb meat stews. Naan is a type of flat bread. People use naan to scoop up stews. Afghans also eat naan topped with sesame seeds or nuts. People eat yogurt plain or use it to flavor other dishes.

Fact!

Muslims do not eat certain foods like pork. They do not drink alcohol. Forbidden foods are called haram. Foods that Muslims can eat are called halal.

Some of Afghanistan's teahouses are open to men only.

Tea is a favorite Afghan drink. Teahouses are popular gathering spots for Afghans. The green or black tea is often flavored with spices.

What is family life like in Afghanistan?

In Afghanistan, relatives often live together or near each other. Families pray, have fun, and often work together.

Men usually make family decisions. They make final decisions on education, marriage, and work for family members.

What are the ethnic backgrounds of people in Afghanistan?

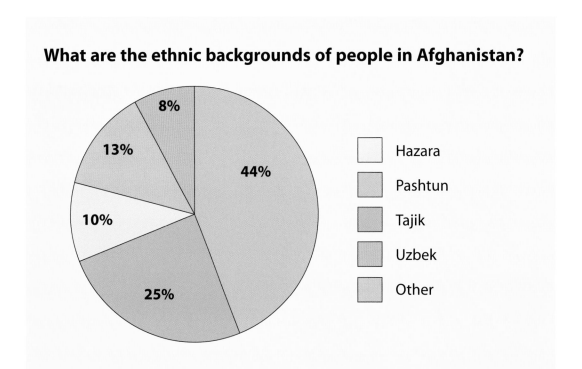

8%

13%

44%

10%

25%

☐ Hazara

☐ Pashtun

☐ Tajik

☐ Uzbek

☐ Other

Afghan families spend much of their free time together.

Some women work outside the home. But women do not spend time with men except their husbands and relatives.

Children help with household chores. Many young boys herd livestock. Young girls help cook and clean.

Afghanistan Fast Facts

Official name:

Transitional Islamic State of Afghanistan

Land area:

250,775 square miles (649,507 square kilometers)

Average annual precipitation (Kabul):

11 inches (28 centimeters)

Average January temperature (Kabul):

29 degrees Fahrenheit (minus 2 degrees Celsius)

Average July temperature (Kabul):

77 degrees Fahrenheit (25 degrees Celsius)

Population:

28,717,213 people

Capital city:

Kabul

Languages:

Pashto and Dari

Other languages are spoken locally.

Natural Resources:

coal, copper, iron ore, natural gas

Religions:

Islamic   *99%*
Other   *1%*

Money and Flag

Money:

Afghanistan's money is the afghani. In early 2004, 1 U.S. dollar equaled 43 afghanis. One Canadian dollar equaled about 32 afghanis.

Flag:

Afghanistan's flag has bands of black, red, and green. Centered on the red band, an emblem shows a mosque and pulpit. Religious leaders speak to their followers from a pulpit. Wheat surrounds the mosque. At the top in Arabic it reads "There is no God but Allah and Muhammad is the Prophet of Allah" and "God is Great."

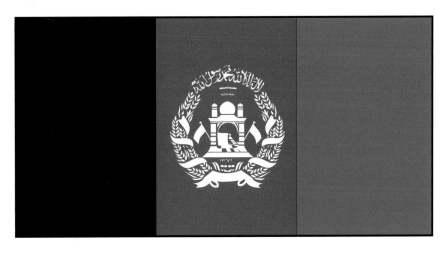

Learn to Speak Pashto

Pashto and Dari are the official languages in Afghanistan. They are written in Arabic script. This way of writing is different from the English alphabet. Below are some words in Pashto written in the English alphabet.

American	Pashto	Pronunciation
hello	assalam u alaikum	(ah-sah-LAM OO ah-LEHK-uhm)
goodbye	de kuday pe aman	(DU KOO-day POO AHM-ahn)
please	lutfan	(LOOT-fahn)
thank you	sta na shukria	(STAH NAH SHOO-kree-uh)
Do you speak English?	Ta pe angrezai pohegy?	(TAH POO ahn-GROO-zay PO-hug-ee?)

Glossary

barley (BAR-lee)—a common type of grain; grains are the seeds of a cereal plant.

constitution (kon-stuh-TOO-shuhn)—the system of laws in a country that state the rights of the people and the powers of the government

ethnic (ETH-nik)—related to a group of people and their culture

fast (FAST)—to give up eating for a period of time

industry (IN-duh-stree)—a single branch of business or trade

Loya Jirga (LOY-uh JER-guh)—a traditional Afghan method of choosing leaders, passing new laws, and settling problems

mosque (MOSK)—a building used by Muslims for worship

Muslim (MUHZ-luhm)—someone who follows the religion of Islam; Islam is a religion whose followers believe in one god, Allah, and that Muhammad is his prophet.

nomad (NOH-mad)—a person who moves from place to place to find food and water, rather than living in one spot

plateau (pla-TOH)—an area of high, flat land

transitional (tran-ZISH-uhn-uhl)—being between two stages

Internet Sites

FactHound offers a safe, fun way to find Internet sites related to this book. All of the sites on FactHound have been researched by our staff.

Here's how:
1. Visit *www.facthound.com*
2. Type in this special code **0736826858** for age-appropriate sites. Or enter a search word related to this book for a more general search.
3. Click on the **Fetch It** button.

FactHound will fetch the best sites for you!

Read More

Banting, Erinn. *Afghanistan: The People.* Lands, Peoples, and Cultures. New York: Crabtree, 2003.

Fordyce, Deborah. *Welcome to Afghanistan.* Welcome to My Country. Milwaukee: Gareth Stevens, 2004.

Knox, Barbara. *Afghanistan.* Many Cultures, One World. Mankato, Minn.: Blue Earth Books, 2004.

Stevens, Kathryn. *Afghanistan.* Faces and Places. Chanhassen, Minn.: Child's World, 2003.

Index